Your Free Gift

I wanted to show my appreciation that you support my work so
I've put together a free gift for you.

Slowcooker Essentials Cookbook

http://thezenfactory.com/51_recipes_free_book/

Just visit the link above to download it now.

I know you will love this gift.

Thanks!

Table of Contents

Introduction

Smoking meats is not a new art. The concept of smoking meat dates back to caveman days when it was necessary for preserving food. As years went by, smoking meat became a popular form of preserving meats for a later date.

Today, meat is smoked to add flavor and carry through with a historically its delicious trend. There are three main types of smoking meat, cold smoking, hot smoking, and smoke roasting.

Cold smoking is used as a flavor enhancer for items such as chicken breasts, beef, pork chops, and salmon, scallops, it and steak. Cold smoking is used for a short duration of time to add flavor to foods that are baked, grilled, steamed, it or sautéed before eating.

Hot smoking exposes the meat to a low, and controlled temperature for a long duration of time. Foods that are hot snow are typically save to eat without further cooking, as long as the internal temperature reaches the recommended degrees Fahrenheit listed by the FDA.

Smoked roasting is a process that refers to smoking combined with either roasting or baking. This smoking message is typically referred to as barbecuing, it baking, or pit roasting. It is typically done over a smoke roast, closed wood fire, or barbecued grill. Essentially, as long as you have a fire and wood chips, and the temperature can RE above 250° F, you can smoke almost any type of meat.

We hope you enjoyed these 51 delicious "Smoked Meat" recipes, and we hope you share them with your family and friends.

Smoking Meats

Smoking meats may take a long time, but this is because while you are cooking meat at a low temperature and slowly in this fashion brings out the true flavor and tender nature of the meat. It can even make toughest cuts of meat succulent and juicy.

There is no reason to spend top dollar on expensive cuts of meat when you can easily smoke a tough brisket and create an amazing work of art for dinner. With the art of smoking meat, even the least appealing of meats can become amazingly tender and deliciously juicy. If you can do this with an unappealing cut of meat, just imagine what you can do with a top quality piece of meat like a Boston butt roast or a gorgeous beef roast.

Even if you have not enjoyed the wonderful flavor of smoked meat before, we guarantee that you will be instantly hooked and it smoking will become a regular part of your family's life. You will be hosting backyard barbecues in no time!

Sweetly Smoked Pork Ribs

(ready in about 5 hours| Serving 10 lbs.)

Ingredients:

- ¼ cup sugar
- ¼ cup salt
- 2 tbsps ground black pepper
- 2 tbsps. Packed brown sugar
- 2 tbsps. Onion powder
- 2 tbsps. Ground white pepper
- 1 tbsp. chili powder
- 1 tbsp. garlic powder
- 1 tbsp. ground cumin
- 1 tbsp. paprika
- 1 cup apple juice
- ¼ cup packed brown sugar
- ¼ cup barbeque sauce
- 10 lbs. pork ribs

Directions:

1. In a small bowl stir sugar, salt, black pepper, 2 tbsps. Brown sugar, onion powder, white pepper, chili powder, garlic powder cumin, and paprika. Take the ribs and rub this dry mixture until well covered. Use plastic wrap to wrap the ribs and let sit in the refrigerator for 30 minutes.
2. Without stacking the ribs place them on the smoker grate.
3. Use wood chips of your choice to bring the smoker to 270 °F. Smoke the ribs for 1 hour.
4. Mix the ¼ cup brown sugar, apple juice, and barbeque sauce to make the rib sauce. Brush the tops of the ribs every 30 minutes with the sauce following the first hour of smoking. Continue cooking the meat until the meat starts to pull back from the bones around 3 to 4 hours. Make sure before the last 30 minutes of cooking time that you brush on sauce.
5. Remove the ribs and wrap in foil to let rest for 15 minutes.

Slow Smoked Ribs

(ready in about 5 hours 20 minutes | Serving 8 to 16)

Ingredients:

- ¼ cup yellow honey mustard
- ¼ cup brown sugar
- ¼ cup onion powder
- 1/3 cup paprika
- 2 tbsps. Dried parsley flakes
- ¼ cup granulate garlic powder
- 1 tbsp. black pepper
- 1-2 tbsp. chipotle chili pepper flakes
- 2 tbsps. Chili powder
- 1 tbsp. black pepper
- 1 tbsp. salt
- 1 tbsp. ground cumin

Directions:

1. Rinse and remove the membrane on the back of the ribs. Lay the ribs top down and use a knife to start peeling the membrane back. After you start peeling it with a knife you should be able to pull it the rest of the way off using your hands.
2. Mix all the ingredients together to make the mustard rub. And coat the ribs completely.
3. Get your smoker preheated to 200 °F. Use a blend of hickory, oak and mesquite wood chips for smoking.
4. Place the ribs on the rack and smoke for 2 hours. Wrap the ribs in heavy foil and return to smoker for 2 more hours. Unwrap and smoke for an additional hour to finish it up.
5. Leave the ribs as is or coat in your favorite sauce.

Apple Smoked Spare Ribs

(ready in about 6 hours | Serving 6)

Ingredients:

- 2 racks pork spareribs
- ½ tsp. cloves
- ½ tsp. cinnamon
- Apple wood chips
- 1/4 tsp. pepper

Barbeque sauce
- ½ cup molasses
- 2 (15 oz.) cans tomato sauce
- 2 tbsp. ground cumin
- 10 cloves garlic
- Fresh ground pepper
- 2 tbsp. dry mustard
- 1/4th tsp. hot pepper flakes
- ½ tsp cinnamon
- ½ cup red wine vinegar

Directions:

1. Rub the ribs with the mixture of cloves, pepper and cinnamon coating the ribs entirely. Place both racks of ribs on the smoking rack
2. Smoke ribs for 6 hours using the apple wood chips. Smoke ribs until tender or internal temp reaches 170 degrees °F.
3. Mix in all the ingredients for the barbeque sauce into a pan and simmer on low heat for 1 hour covered. You have to add the vinegar to taste while occasionally stirring. Allow the sauce to simmer for an additional 15 minutes. Place in the refrigerator to cool.

Barbequed Smoked Ribs

(ready in about 3 hours 30 minutes | Serving 3 racks)

Ingredients:

- 2 tbsps. Packed dark brown sugar
- 3 tbsps. Salt
- 2 tbsps. Smoked paprika
- 2 tbsps. Chili powder
- 1 tsp. cayenne pepper
- 1 ½ tsps. fresh ground black pepper
- 1 tsp. garlic powder
- 1 tsp. ground cumin
- 1 tsp. ground mustard
- 3 (2 to 3 lb.) full racks pork ribs
- 3 cups apple wood chip, soaked in water
- 3 tbsps. Vegetable oil
- 2 cups bourbon-bacon barbecue sauce
- 8 qt. lump charcoal

Directions:

1. Mix the sugar, salt, and spices into a small bowl.
2. Place the ribs meat side down. Use a sharp knife and cut the silver membrane while pulling it back. After you get it started you should be able to pull the rest off.
3. Rub the vegetable oil over the ribs coating them completely. Sprinkle the mix of spices over the coated ribs. Lay the ribs out over the pan and use plastic wrap to cover. Place the ribs in the refrigerator for 30 minutes to 8 hours. Remove the pan of ribs from the refrigerator and let sit until they come back to room temperature.
4. Fill the charcoal grill with charcoal and get them started. When the charcoal becomes grayed over place the wood chips in the middle. Make sure the grill is preheated to 250 °F.
5. Place the ribs on the rack meat side up and smoke for 30 minutes. Flip the ribs over and cook for 30 minutes. Add the rest of the wood chips and flip the ribs meat side back up. Cook for another 15 minutes. Slather your barbeque sauce on the ribs and cook for an additional 15 minutes.
6. Remove the ribs and serve.

Memphis Hickory Smoked Ribs (beef or pork)
(ready in about 14 hours 25 minutes | Serving 4 to 6)

Ingredients:

- ¾ cup sugar
- 1 ½ cups paprika
- 3 ¾ tbsps. onion powder
- 2 (4 lbs. each) rack beef ribs
- 2 (3 lbs. each) rack pork ribs
- 1 cup water
- 2 cups ketchup
- 5 tbsps. Light brown sugar
- ½ cup apple cider vinegar
- 1 tbsp. lemon juice
- 5 tbsps. Sugar
- ½ tbsp. onion powder
- ½ tbsp. ground black pepper
- 1 tbsp. Worcestershire sauce

- ½ tbsp. ground mustard

Directions:

1. Mix the sugar paprika and onion powder into a bowl.
2. Clean the ribs by removing the membrane with a knife.
3. Coat your ribs generously with your dry rub sugar mixture. Wrap the ribs in plastic wrap and place in the refrigerator for 8 hours.
4. Preheat your grill to 250 °F using charcoal. When the charcoals gray over place a handful of hickory wood chips on the coals.
5. Place the beef ribs meat side down on the grill in indirect heat. Smoke for 2 hours adding coals as needed. Also add a handful of wood chips every hour. Turn and cook for an additional 45 minutes.
6. Place the pork ribs on the grill and smoke for 3 hours. Flip the ribs over and smoke an additional hour. Follow the steps of the beef ribs.
7. Mix the last 10 ingredients together to create the barbecue sauce.
8. Coat the ribs with the sauce generously.

3-2-1 Smoking Smoked Ribs
(ready in about 3 hours | Serving 1 rack)

Ingredients:

- 3 tsp. salt
- ½ cup sugar
- 3 tsp. fresh ground pepper
- 2 tsp. Chipotle pepper seasoning
- 1 tsp. Sriracha seasoning
- 2 tsp. garlic powder

Directions:

1. Clean your rack of ribs by removing the membrane with a sharp knife.
2. Mix the ingredients in a bowl and coat your ribs generously from top to bottom.

3. Preheat your smoker to 220 °F. Place your hickory wood chips in the smoker and wait until the smoke starts rolling.
4. Place your ribs meat side up on the smoker grill to smoke for 3 hours placing a handful of wood chips on every hour.
5. Remove the ribs from the heat and wrap them in heavy foil adding in a splash or apple juice. Wrap the ribs well but loose enough to allow for steam flow.
6. Place the ribs back in the smoker for 2 hours again adding a handful of wood chips every hour.
7. Remove from the heat and unwrap the ribs. Place the ribs back on the grill for 1 more hour. Add any glaze of your choice if desired. My store bought barbecue of choice is Sweet Baby Rays.

Last Meal Smoked Ribs
(ready in about 6 hours | Serving 2)

Ingredients:

- ¾ cup sugar
- ¾ cup packed dark brown sugar
- ¼ cup garlic powder
- ½ cup paprika
- 2 tbsps. Ground ginger powder
- 2 tbsps. Ground black pepper
- 2 tsps. Rosemary powder
- 2 tbsps. Onion powder
- 1 tbsp. vegetable oil
- ¾ tsps. Salt
- 1 cup barbecue sauce of your choice

Directions:

1. Mix the first 8 ingredients to make the seasoning in a bowl. This will make 3 cups of seasoning (not all is needed).
2. Use a sharp knife to start removing the membrane off the back of the ribs. After you have it started remove the rest using your hands.
3. Dry rub the ribs with salt, wrap with plastic wrap and place in the fridge for 1 to 2 hours.
4. Rub the ribs down with vegetable oil and sprinkle the seasoning mix on as desired.
5. Preheat your smoker to 225 °F and add a handful of wood chips of your choice. When the smoke starts to roll place your rack of ribs meat side up on indirect heat. Add another handful of wood chips every 30 minutes. Smoke for 3 to 4 hours and repeat adding wood chips.
6. You can check to see if they are done by holding the ribs with tongs and bounce them lightly if the surface of the ribs crack.

Smoked Pork Spare Ribs
(ready in about 12 hours | Serving 6)

Ingredients:

- 2 Tbsps. Chili powder
- ½ cup packed brown sugar
- 1 tbsp. black pepper
- 1 tbsp. paprika
- 2 tsp. onion powder
- 2 tbsps. Garlic powder
- 2 tsps. Ground cumin
- 2 tsps. Salt
- 1 tsp. jalapeno seasoning salt
- 1 tsp. ground cinnamon
- 1 tsp. cayenne pepper
- ¾ cup apple cider vinegar
- 1 cup apple cider
- 1 tbsp. garlic powder
- 1 tbsp. onion powder

- 1 jalapeno pepper, finely chopped
- 2 tbsps. Lemon juice
- Kosher salt and ground black pepper to taste
- 3 tbsps. Hot pepper sauce
- 2 cups wood chips, soaked
- 6 lbs. pork spareribs

Directions:

1. Place the first 11 ingredients in to a bowl and mix together and rub the mixture on the ribs. Make sure you coat them generously, cover with plastic wrap and refrigerate for up to 4 hours.
2. Preheat your grill to 250 °F and wait for charcoal to gray over
3. Mix the remaining ingredients in a medium sized bowl.
4. Place 2 handfuls of your desired wood chips on the charcoal. Lay the ribson the grill meat side up. Close the top on the grill and cook for 3 ½ to 4 hours. Add any additional coals as needed. Coat your ribs with the barbecue sauce adding a handful of woodchips every hour. Try to maintain the temperature of your grill at 225 °F. The ribs will be done when the meat will have pulled away from the bone.

Baby's Got Back Ribs
(ready in about 6 hours | Serving 2 racks)

Ingredients:

- 1/3 cup yellow mustard
- 1 tbsp. Worcestershire sauce
- ½ cup apple juice (divided)
- ½ cup packed dark brown sugar
- 1/3 cup honey, warmed
- Barbecue sauce of your choice.

Directions:

1. Clean the membrane off the ribs using a sharp knife. Once you have the membrane started, use your hands to pull the rest of the membrane off.
2. Combine the ¼ cup apple juice, mustard and Worcestershire sauce into a small bowl.

3. Coat your ribs with the sauce and sprinkle on your favorite rub.
4. Preheat your smoker to 225 °F and add wood chips of your choice.
5. Place your ribs on the smoker grill for 3 hours meat side up. Remove from heat and place on heavy duty foil pulling the foil sides up so that it will hold some liquid.
6. Pour half of the honey on the ribs, sprinkle half of the brown sugar over the top and add some apple juice. Place another sheet of foil over the ribs and crimp the edges to keep the juices in and allow the ribs to smoke.
7. Return the ribs to the grill to cook for 2 hours.
8. Remove the foil and brush on the barbecue sauce of your choice.
9. Return the ribs to the heat and cook for your additional and last hour.

Simple Beef Ribs

(ready in about 3 hours | Serving 6)

Ingredients:

- ¼ cup dill pickle juice
- 1 cup prepared yellow mustard
- 2 tbsps. Worcestershire sauce
- ¼ cup red wine vinegar
- 1 tsp. granulated garlic
- 2 tbsps. Soy sauce
- 1 tsp. ground ginger
- 2 tbsps. Coarse ground black pepper
- 2 tbsps. Sea salt
- 2 tsps. White sugar
- 1 tbsp. granulated garlic.
- 6 (4 or 5 inch long) beef short ribs

Directions:

1. Clean the membrane from the ribs using a sharp knife.
2. Mix the first 7 ingredients into a bowl creating a mustard mixture. Slather the mixture onto the ribs coating generously
3. Mix the last 4 seasonings into a small bowl and sprinkle over the ribs
4. Preheat your smoker to 230 °F and add wood chips of desired flavor.
5. When smoke starts to form oil the smoker rack and place the ribs on indirect heat meat side up. Smoke for 1 ½ hours adding a handful of woodchips every half hour. Turn over the ribs and cook for an additional 45 minutes. Turn once more until internal temperatures reach 185 °F
6. Remove and let rest for 10 to 15 minutes.

Divinely Smoked Salmon
(ready in about 29 hours 30 minutes | Serving 4)

Ingredients:

- Salmon fillets: 2 large
- Black peppercorns 1 tsp, crushed
- Coarse salt: 1 tsp
- Juice and zest of 2 limes of any kind
- Olive oil: 2 tbsp

Directions:

Brine Recipe:

1. ¾ cup of plain salt (Iodine-free Salt) and 20 cups of water
2. Add 4 cups of water in a bowl. Heat water till it's lukewarm. Add only 2 ½ tbsp. of salt to make Brine and keep stirring till

it dissolves. Once dissolved, add the warm water to the cold water (16 cups) along with the remaining salt.

3. Rinse the salmon thoroughly with salt water and place it in brine for at-least 20mins and note that the entire salmon covered with brine. (Place the salmon skin side down)

4. Remove the salmon from brine and wash both the sides gently with cold water to remove any traces of salt over it. Use any kind of paper towel to dry it up.

5. Place the salmon over a wire-rack (if any) for at least 2 hours. (This will help to form lines/pellicle)

Main recipe:

1. Pre-heat the Electric Smoker to 200-225 degrees F. keep monitoring it during smoke time.

2. On an aluminum foil, place the brine salmon and cut the foil around it approximately a little bigger than the salmon.

3. Mix zest of lime, lime juice, peppercorns, salt, herbs and olive oil in a small bowl. Add this seasoning mix and coat the salmon well.

4. Keep the salmon on the smoker-rack and smoke to a temperature of 140 degrees F with the help of a meat-thermometer.

5. Squeeze half lemon juice and a bit of coarse salt over the salmon.

6. Serve hot, cold or chilled in refrigerator.

Perfectly Smoked Salmon

(ready in about 45 min | Serving 2)

Ingredients:

- 2 piece of salmon fillets
- 2 table spoon of lemon zest
- 3 fresh lime concentrates
- 1 tablespoon freshly chopped thyme leaves
- Extra-virgin oil (add as per your convenience)
- Sea salt or coarse salt for taste

Directions:

Preparation:

Time taken for preparation is 3 hours

How to make brine:

1. Heat 3-4 cups of water and bring it to the lukewarm temperature. Add 3 tablespoon of salt and mix it well till the salt dissolves in the water. Again add this dissolved lukewarm salt water to a bowl of cold water (10-12 cups). Again add around 3/4 cup of salt into the mixture. The brine is ready
2. Rinse the Salmon fillets in the cold water and then drown the fillets in this brine for around 20 minutes.

Smoking the Salmon:

1. If you have an electric smoker, then the temperature of the smoker should be set around 200-225 degree Fahrenheit. Always use the bottom vents to adjust the temperature and keep open the top vents. If your smoker don't have any vent then make a small gap by loosening the cock of the vent so that there is a minimal exhaust.
2. Take the fillets out of the brine and keep them on the aluminum foil and design the foil as per the fillets. If needed you can spray a considerable amount of oil spray to avoid any stickiness on the racks of the smoker.
3. Take 2 tablespoon of lemon zest in a bowl, pour the concentrated lime juice and mix them well. Add the chopped thyme leaves, oil, pepper and salt for taste. Mix the ingredients well and apply well on the smoked salmons.
4. Again place back the coated salmons back in the smoker until the meat temperature shows around 140 -150 degree F.
5. Remove them from the smoker (make sure it is perfectly smoked, don't overcook the salmon)
6. Squeeze half a lime onto the cooked salmons, sprinkle a little sea salt and your perfectly smoked salmon is ready to eat.

Creamy Pasta with Smoked Salmon
(ready in about 30 hours | Serving 8)

Ingredients:

- 1 cured ham
- 1 cup mustard
- Spices to your liking
- Hickory wood chips

Directions:

1. Time taken for preparation: Just 30 minutes.
2. Heat water with a pinch of salt in a large pot.
3. When the water starts to boil, add the pasta and cook for good 10 minutes till the pasta turns big and soft.

4. Take a frying pan a melt the butter in it. Add the chopped onions and sauté until it becomes tender.
5. Add the flour and garlic powder and mix it well. Pour the milk to the mixture and stir it well.
6. Once it reaches the boiling point, add the grated cheese and stir it until the sauce becomes smooth and creamy.
7. Add the mushrooms and peas to the mixture and cook it for 5 minutes.
8. Add the smoked salmon and cook for 2 more minutes. Your sauce it ready.
9. Serve pasta in the dish and pour the sauce and enjoy the creamy pasta with smoked salmon.

Alfredo Sauce Pasta with Smoked Salmon

(ready in about 20 min | Serving 4)

Ingredients:

- 2 tablespoon of onion chopped
- ¼ cup of butter
- ½ pound smoked and chopped salmon
- ½ cup of diced tomatoes
- 2 tablespoons chopped fresh parsley
- 500 ml whipped cream
- Black pepper and salt to taste

Directions:

1. Melt the butter in a large pan, add chopped onions and sauté till it turns tender.
2. Add Salmon and sauté at medium low flame for around 2 minutes.
3. Add cream by continuous stirring until it thickens
4. Sauce should be very thick once you have added all the cream
5. Add tomato and parsley and season with pepper.

Smoked Salmon Fried Rice

(ready in about 35 min | Serving 8)

Ingredients:

- 3 cups of white rice grains
- 5-6 cups of water (as needed for the rice and ingredients to cook)
- 3 table-spoon of cooking oil
- 2 eggs whisked
- 1/2 cup onion finely chopped
- 1 chopped green onion
- 4 ounces of chopped salmon
- 1/2 cup peas
- Salt and pepper to taste

Directions:

1. Heat water in a thick bottom pan, add rice and bring the rice to boil. Cook in a low flame until the rice is tender. Once done, keep it aside.
2. Heat 2 tablespoon of cooking oil in a large frying pan, pour in the whisked egg and stir fry it till it becomes scrambled. Empty it in a bowl.
3. Take the same frying pan and heat 1 table spoon of oil, add the chopped onions and the green onion and stir it till golden brown.
4. Add salmon, cooked rice, cup of peas and scrambled egg and toss it neat and gently until all the ingredients are mixed well and blended evenly. Keep cooking and tossing occasionally.
5. Add salt and pepper and toss the mixture and your special fried salmon rice is ready to eat.

Salmon with Dill Eggs Benedict

(ready in about 20 minutes | Serving 2)

Ingredients:

- 4 tablespoon softened butter
- 4 eggs
- 2 tablespoons fresh dill
- 2 English muffins (split and toasted)
- 1 teaspoon lemon zest
- 4 ounces smoked and sliced salmon
- 4-5 small fresh dill springs
- 1 teaspoon of vinegar
- Cayenne pepper, black pepper and salt to taste.

Directions:

1. Take an empty bowl, add the softened butter, lemon zest and dill and mix them thoroughly. Then add salt, black pepper and cayenne pepper and again mixed and set aside.
2. Take a large sauce pan and 3-4 cups of water and bring it to boil over high heat.
3. Reduce the heat and add some vinegar and salt
4. Break the egg into the bowl and slowly pour it into the hot water. Repeat the same step for the remaining eggs. Let the egg boil in water till the yolks are thickened. Let it remain for around 5 minutes and then slowly remove the eggs and place it into the kitchen towel to remove excess water.
5. Spread the prepared butter mix into the muffin slits. Top it with the salmon layers and poached egg. Repeat the same for the remaining muffins. Sprinkle with salt and black pepper to taste and add some dill springs.

Smoker Salmon Chowder

(ready in about 1 hour 45 minutes| Serving 8)

Ingredients:

- 1 tablespoon olive oil
- 5-6 tablespoon of chopped onions.
- 2 tablespoons of butter
- 1 teaspoon of dried thyme
- Half teaspoon paprika
- 250 grams of smoked salmon cut into tiny pieces
- Half tablespoon of garlic chopped
- Half cup chopped celery
- Half cup all-purpose flour
- 5-6 cups of veg broth or chicken broth
- 3-4 potatoes peeled and cubed
- 1 teaspoon dried dill weed

- 1 teaspoon dried tarragon
- 5-6 tablespoon of white wine
- 1 cup of mixture of milk and cream (half n half)
- A pinch of hot sauce
- Salt and pepper to taste

Directions:

1. Take a large pot and melt butter in it, olive oil, onion, garlic and celery and cook for good 8 minutes till the onion turns golden brown
2. Sprinkle a little flour and stir well and make it a dry mixture
3. Add chicken broth and stir till the mixture thickens into a paste
4. Add the chopped potatoes, dill, tarragon, thyme and the pinch and paprika and cook with the medium heat covering the pot for 15 minutes
5. After 15 minutes, add in salmon, wine and lemon juice and the pinch of hot sauce and mix well.
6. Add salt and pepper to taste and cook uncovered for 10 minutes.
7. Add the milk and cream mixture and continue to cook in low flame for 30 more minutes by stirring occasionally. Make a note that the recipe should not boil after adding half and half.

Smoked Salmon Salad with Asparagus

(ready in about 25 min | Serving 8)

Ingredients:

- Fresh Asparagus cut into tiny pieces – 1 pound
- 4 tablespoon of pecans broken into pieces
- 2 red head leafy lettuce rinsed and torn
- ½ cup green peas thawed
- 150-200 grams of smoked salmon (1/4 pound)
- 4 tablespoon of olive oil
- 2 tablespoons of concentrated lemon juice
- 1 teaspoon of mustard
- Salt and pepper for taste.

Directions:

1. Fill a cooking pot of water and bring it to boil.
2. Place the asparagus into the boiling water pot and cook for 5 minutes, remove the excess water and keep the tender boiled asparagus aside.
3. Take a frying pan and add the peas over the medium flame and cook for 5 minutes and stir continuously
4. Take a large bowl, put in all the ingredients like asparagus, pecans, red lettuce, salmon and peas and toss well.
5. In a small separate bowl, add in olive oil, lemon juice, mustard, salt and pepper. Add the mixture and toss the salad well.

Smoked Salmon Frittata

(ready in about 1 hour | Serving 4)

Ingredients:

- Olive oil – 4 tablespoon
- 2 tablespoon of chopped onions
- 4 ounces of pepper smoked salmon
- 7-8 olives chopped
- 6 whisked eggs whisked with 2 tablespoon milk and 2 tablespoon cream
- 8 ounce of cubed packaged cheese.

Directions:

1. You would need an oven preheated for 350 degrees Fahrenheit
2. Take a micro-wave safe pan and heat olive oil. Add onion and sprinkle a little salt and pepper. Sauté it until it's tender.
3. Add the salmon and olives and cook for good 3-4 minutes with continues stirring.
4. Pour the mixture of whisked eggs with milk and cream onto this recipe.
5. Add the cheese over the top evenly and cook over medium heat without touching until the cheese melts and the top becomes strong.
6. Place the pan in pre-heated oven and bake for 20 minutes until it is puffed and cooked. The smoked salmon frittata is ready.

Smoked Salmon Pesto Pasta
(ready in about 30 minutes | Serving 4)

Ingredients:

- Smoked salmon cut into tiny piece (5 ounces)
- 3 tablespoon of tomato paste.
- ½ cup of chopped onions
- 1 clove of crushed garlic
- 2 cups of finely sliced mushrooms
- ¾ cup of basil pesto sauce
- 3 tablespoon of tomato paste
- 2 tablespoons olive oil
- 1 tablespoon chopped fresh basil
- ¼ cup of water
- 250 grams (8 ounces) of spaghetti

Directions:

1. In a large pot of boiling water cook the spaghettis until its tender.
2. In the frying pan, heat the olive oil. Add onion, mushrooms and garlic and sauté till tender.
3. Add the smoked salmon, tomato paste, pesto sauce, fresh basil and water and cook gently for good 10 minutes
4. Serve the Spaghetti and top it with the prepared sauce mixture and your recipe is ready to relish.

Cajun Smoked Beer Chicken
(ready in about 4 hours 30 minutes | Servings 4 to 6)

Ingredients:

- 3 to 4 lb. Chicken
- ½ onion, chopped
- 3 cloves garlic
- Beer of your choice

Injection Ingredients
- 2 tbsps. Tony Chachere's seasoning
- ½ cup melted butter
- 1 tsp. garlic powder

Rub Ingredients
- Tony Chachere's seasoning
- Olive oil

Mop Ingredients
- ½ cup olive oil
- Spray bottle
- 1 cup of apple cider

Directions:

1. Mix all the ingredients for the injection in a bowl and whisk well.
2. Use an injector and evenly distribute the injection to all parts of the chicken.
3. Use the olive oil to rub down the chicken and rub the now oiled chicken with the seasoning rub.
4. Take the beer and drink the first half of it. Widen the top and place your onion and garlic inside.
5. Sit the bird upright placing the can inside the chicken.
6. Get your smoker preheated to 250 °F and use hickory wood chips to smoke with.
7. Use the ingredients for the mop mixture and mix them in a spray bottle by shaking them.
8. Place your beer filled chicken on the smoker spraying it down with the mop spray. Continue to spray every 30 minutes keeping it moist.
9. Cook the chicken for 3 to 4 hours or until internal temperatures meet 175 °F

Lemon Lime Chicken

(ready in about 4 hour 30 min | Serving 4-6)

Ingredients:

- 4 cups Lemon-lime tequila mix
- 1 (5 lb.) Whole chicken
- 1 tbsp. onion powder
- 1 tbsp. garlic powder
- 1 tbsp. cayenne lemon pepper

Directions:

1. Combine tequila mix and seasonings in a large reseal able plastic bag with the whole chicken. Seal the bagged chicken and place it in the refrigerator to marinade for 6 hours.
2. Preheat your smoker to 250 °F
3. Remove the chicken from the refrigerator and remove it from the bad. Place it on the preheated grill.
4. Lightly coat the chicken with lemon pepper.

5. Smoke the chicken for 4 hours adding a handful of wood chips every half hour until internal temperatures reach at least 175 °F.

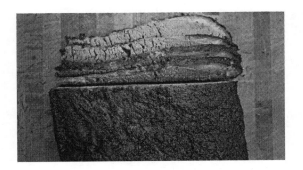

Smoked Brisket
(ready in about 6 hours | Servings 8 to 10)

Ingredients:

- 1 – 12 pound beef brisket, fat trimmed down to ¼ inch thickness
- 1/3 cup salt
- 1/3 cup ground black pepper

Directions:

1. Mix salt and pepper in a small bowl. Season the meat while it is still wet so that the seasoning sticks to the meat well.
2. Allow the meat to sit for at least 1 hour at room temperature so that the seasoning has time to flavor the meat.

Prepare Grill

3. Fill the smoker with charcoal. Allow to burn for approximately 10 to 15 minutes or until the coals are covered with a thin layer of ash.
4. Pour the charcoal into one side of the grill. Place three chunks of wood next to the coals. This will allow the wood to catch slowly and smolder.
5. Check the coals every 45 minutes and add to the fire when your grill can no longer maintain a temperature of 250 degrees F.
6. It should not take more than 4 to 6 chimneyfuls of coals to cook the brisket.
7. Flip the brisket and rotate it every three hours. When it is finished cooking, the meat should be tender, but not falling apart. A meat thermometer inserted into the thickest portion of the meat should read between 195 degrees F – 205 degrees F, which should take 10 to 12 hours.

Texas Barbecue Ribs

(ready in about 6 hours 30 minutes| Servings 4)

Ingredients:

- Honey
- Brown sugar
- 11 oz. chili powder
- 1/3 cup brown sugar
- 2 tbsps. Garlic powder
- 2 tbsps. Seasoning salt
- 2 tbsps. Cayenne
- 2 tbsps. Onion powder
- 2 tbsps. Paprika
- 1 tbsp. cracked black pepper

Directions:

1. Preheat your smoker to 250 °F using hickory or pecan woodchips, which had been soaked in water.
2. Rub your ribs down with your dry rub made of the ingredients and allow to sit for one hour.
3. Place the ribs on indirect heat for 2 ½ hours.

4. Place the ribs in some foil and cover with honey and brown sugar.
5. Cook for 2 ½ to 3 hours longer and rib bones pull out easily.

Turkey Times
(ready in about 7 hours | Servings 8 to 10)

Ingredients:

- Salt, to taste
- Red pepper flakes, to lightly coat
- 4 cloves garlic, smashed
- 2 jalapeno peppers, sliced
- 13 to 15 pound turkey
- 1 tbsp. chili powder
- 1 tbsp. ground coriander
- 2 tsp. ground cumin
- 1 tsp packed brown sugar, dark brown
- 1 tsp. garlic powder
- 1 tsp rosemary, fresh and chopped
- 1 tsp chopped thyme, fresh
- Ground black pepper, to taste
- 2 tbsp. mayonnaise
- 1 pound sliced bacon, preferably applewood smoked

Directions:

1. Create brine by combining the 1 cup salt, pepper flakes, garlic, jalapenos and 2 quarts hot water in a large pot. Stir the mixture until the salt is dissolved. Place the turkey in the mixture breast side down. Add enough cold water to fully submerge the turkey. Cover the pot and refrigerate for 12 hours. Drain the turkey, rinse and pat dry.
2. Soak 2 large bags of mesquite and 2 large bags of Applewood in water for 1 hour.
3. Create spice blend by combining chili powder, coriander, cumin brown sugar, garlic powder, rosemary, thyme 1 tbsp. salt, and 2 tsp pepper. Loosen the skin of the turkey with your fingers gently. Rub the meat with mayonnaise.
4. Rub the spice blend all over the skin of the bird. Put the turkey in a large roasting pan breast side up.
5. Lay ¾ of the bacon over the breast of the bird overlapping slices and securing with toothpicks.
6. Wrap the legs with the remaining portion of the bacon, secure it with toothpicks.
7. Drain the water from the woodchips and prepare the smoker per manufacturer's directions. Preheat smoker box to 210 degrees F. Put turkey, still in the disposable pan, on the smoker grates. Cover and cook for 6 to 7 hours, or until a meat thermometer registers 190 degrees in the thickest portion of the turkey.
8. Make sure to add a few handfuls of soaked wood chips every hour to maintain the required level of smoke. If the bacon is browning too quickly, cover the turkey loosely with foil.
9. Allow to rest for 30 minutes before removing bacon and carving. Chop up the bacon and sprinkle it on top of the carved turkey.

Smoked Chili
(ready in about 4 hours 30 min | Serving 6)

Ingredients:

- 5 pounds ground beef
- 2 tbsp. canola oil
- 1 large onion, chopped
- 1 tbsp. garlic, minced
- 2 heaping tbsp. all-purpose flour
- 28 ounce can diced tomatoes
- 2 six ounce cans tomato paste
- 4 ounces of aged cheese
- 2 tbsp. brown sugar
- 1 tsp ground cinnamon
- 2 beef bouillon cubes
- ½ tsp cayenne powder
- SYD Hot rub, to taste
- Chili spice dunk
- 3 heaping tbsp. mild chili powder
- 2 heaping tbsp. paprika
- 2 tbsp. ground cumin

Directions:

1. Sauté the ground beef in large sauce pan with a little canola oil until the beef. Season with SYD hot rub to taste. Transfer the beef to a cast iron pot with a slotted spoon to prevent too much grease transfer.
2. Drain off any fat that did make it to the pot leaving only 4 tbsp. of fat in the previous pan. Add in onions and sauté until they are translucent. Add in chopped garlic and cook for a few more minutes. Use a slotted spoon to transfer the onion and garlic mixture to the pot you are cooking the chili in.
3. Whisk in two tbsp. of flour to the oil under a medium-low heat to make a roux. Add a little more oil if needed to create the right consistency. The result should feel like uncooked pancake batter and should be light brown.
4. Once the roux is light brown, turn the heat up and add ½ cup of water at a time. To whisk the roux into gravy. Once you have reached the consistency of gravy, stop adding water.
5. Add in the canned tomatoes, tomato paste, block of cheese, brown sugar, cinnamon, crumbled bouillon cubes, cayenne, salt and pepper. Pour the entire amount Pour the entire mixture into the pan you cooked your ground beef. If you're not going to smoke your chili on the pit, you can transfer the chili to a crockpot or stove pot to simmer.
6. Add half of the spice dunk mixture and mix thoroughly. Place the pot on the pit at 250 to 300 degrees F. Smoke the chili uncovered for several hours. Stir the chili every hour and add more water as needed.
7. Add the remaining ½ of the spice dunk mixture 15 minutes before you plan to eat the chili. Taste the chili before serving and adjust spices.

Coffee Coated Texas Barbecue Brisket
(ready in about 7 hours | Serving 18)

Ingredients:

- 6 cups oak or hickory wood chips
- 1 tbsp. ground coffee
- 1 tbsp. kosher salt
- 1 tbsp. dark brown sugar
- 2 tsp. paprika
- 2 tspanchoChile powder
- 1 tsp garlic powder
- 1 tsp onion powder
- 1 tsp ground cumin
- 1 tsp freshly ground black pepper
- 1 brisket that weighs 4 ½ to 5 pounds, about 3 inches thick.

Directions:

1. Soak the woodchips in water for at least 1 hour, drain completely.
2. Combine the coffee and following 8 ingredients in a bowl. Pat the brisket dry and rub with mixture.
3. Remove the grill rack and set aside, prepare for indirect grilling. This means that you will be heating one side to high and the other side will not have any heat. Use a knife and pierce the bottom of a disposable pan several times. Place this pan on the heated side of the grill. Add 1 ½ cups wood chips to the pan. Place a second disposable pan on the unheated side of the grill. Pour 2 cups of water in the pan. Allow to sit for 15 minutes or until the woodchips are smoking. Reduce the heat to medium low and maintain a temperature around 225 degrees F.
4. Place the grill rack on the grill and place the brisket in a small roasting pan. Place it on the unheated side of the grill rack. Close the lid and allow to cook for 6 hours, or until the meat thermometer reaches 195 degrees F in the thickest portion of the meat.
5. Ensure that you add fresh wood chips after 4 hours. Cover the pan with foil for the last 2 hours. Remove from the grill and allow to stand for 30 minutes, still covered.
6. Unwrap the brisket, reserving juices. Trim the fat from the brisket and use a large zip-top plastic bag inside of a 4 cup glass measuring cup. Pour juices through a sieve into a bag. Discard solids. Allow drippings to stand for 10 minutes. Seal the bag. Cut off one corner of the bag and allow the drippings to drain into a bowl. Before the fat reaches the opening, stop the flow. Discard fat. Cut the brisket across the grain into thin slices. Serve with the juices.

Texas Style Barbecue Chicken

(ready in about 50 minutes | Serving 8)

Ingredients:

- 8 boneless breast halves
- 3 tbsp. brown sugar
- 1 tbsp. ground paprika
- 1 tsp salt
- 1 tsp dry mustard
- ½ tsp chili powder
- ¼ c distilled white vinegar
- 1/8 tsp cayenne pepper
- 2 tbsp. Worcestershire sauce
- ½ cup tomato – vegetable juice cocktail
- ½ c ketchup
- ¼ c water
- 2 cloves garlic, minced

Directions:

1. Preheat oven to 350 degrees F.
2. Place chicken breasts in a single layer in a 9 x 13 inch baking dish.
3. In a medium bowl, mix together the brown sugar, paprika, salt, dry mustard, chili powder, vinegar, cayenne pepper, Worcestershire sauce, vegetable juice cocktail, ketchup, water and garlic. Pour sauce over the chicken breasts.
4. Bake uncovered for 35 minutes in the oven. Remove the chicken breasts, shred with a fork and put back in sauce. Bake for an additional 10 minutes so that the chicken can soak up more flavor. Serve on a bed of rice with freshly ground pepper.

Filet Mignon with Herb butter and Texas Toast
(ready in about 45 min | Serving 4)

Ingredients:

- 1 tbsp. butter, softened
- 3 tsp extra-virgin olive oil, divided
- 1 tbsp. minced fresh chives
- 1 tbsp. capers, rinsed and chopped
- 3 tsp minced fresh marjoram, divided
- 1 tsp lemon juice
- ¾ tsp salt, divided
- 1 tbsp. minced rosemary
- 2 cloves garlic (1 minced, 1 peeled and halved)

- 1 pound filet mignon, bout 1 ½ inches thick, trimmed and cut into 4 pieces.
- 4 slices bread of your choice
- 4 cups watercress, trimmed and chopped

Directions:

1. Preheat a grill to high.
2. Mash butter in a small bowl with the back of a spoon until it is soft and creamy. Stir in 2 teaspoons oil until it is combined. Add chives, capers, 1 tsp marjoram, ½ tsplemon zest, lemon juice, ½tsp salt and ¼ tsp pepper. Cover and place in the freezer to chill.
3. Combine the following in a medium bowl: 1 tsp oil, 2 tsp marjoram, ½ tsp lemon zest, ¼ tsp salt and pepper, rosemary, and minced garlic. Rub on both sides of the bread with the halved clove of garlic. Discard garlic.
4. Grill the steak for 5 minutes per side for a medium rare doneness. Grill the bread until lightly toasted, 30 seconds to 1 minute per side.
5. Place one piece of toast n each serving plate. Top with watercress and top with steak.
6. Spread the herb butter on top of the steaks and let rest for 5 minutes before cutting or serving.

Texas Squealer Burger
(ready in about 50 minutes | Serving 6 to 8)

Ingredients:

- 1 ½ pounds ground beef
- 12 slices flavored bacon, uncooked
- 1 ½ tbsp. grill seasoning
- 1 tsp garlic powder
- 1 tbsp. minced dried onion
- ¼ c Worcestershire sauce
- Salt and pepper to taste

Directions:

1. Chop bacon finely with a sharp knife. Slice it in half and then into strips. Dice the bacon finely.

2. Mix all ingredients in a large bowl and add bacon to the mixture.
3. Form patties and put them in the freezer for 30 minutes before grilling.
4. Grill patties for about 5 minutes on each side. Allow them to rest for 5 minutes before cutting or serving.
5. Top burgers with cheese and your favorite toppings.

Smoked Cedar Plank Salmon

(ready in about 30 minutes | Serving 1)

Ingredients:

- 4 tbsp vegetable oil
- 6 tbsp bourbon
- 2 tbsp soy sauce
- 1 tsp ground ginger
- 2 tbsp light brown sugar
- Ground black pepper, to taste
- 2 pound fillet of salmon
- 1 tsp fresh squeezed lemon juice

Directions:

6. In a medium bowl, combine all of your dry ingredients. In another bowl, blend wet ingredients. Mix together to create marinade.
7. Remove any pin bones that the butcher left in the salmon fillet.
8. Place the salmon in a shallow dish or bowl. Pour marinade over the salmon and allow to sit covered with saran wrap for at least 20 minutes.
9. Preheat your cedar plank while your fillet marinades. When your plank is preheated, lift the lid and place the fish skin side down on the plan. Place the lid back on the hot smoker for about 10 minutes, or until the fillet is done to your specifications.
10. Transfer the marinade into a small sauce pan. Bring the mixture to a simmer and allow it to reduce to ½ of what it originally started as. Remove the glaze from the heat and add in lemon juice. Drizzle the mixture over the salmon right before serving.

Smooth-Smoked Ham

(ready in about 5 hours | Serving 12)

Ingredients:

- 1 cured ham
- 1 cup mustard
- Spices to your liking
- Hickory wood chips

Directions:

1. Apply the mustard in a thin layer over the outside of the ham. Rub on any spice mix you may want making sure to cover the ham entirely.

2. Heat smoker to 225 degrees °F and apply hickory wood chips. Wait till the smoker begins to smoke.
3. Place the ham in the smoker and let smoke for 3 to 5 hours.

Apple Smoked Spare Ribs

(ready in about 6 hours | Serving 6)

Ingredients:

- 2 slabs pork spareribs
- ½ tsp. ground cloves
- ½ tsp. cinnamon
- Apple wood chips
- 1/4th tsp. pepper

Barbeque sauce
- ½ cup molasses
- 2 (15 oz.) cans tomato sauce
- 2 tbsp. ground cumin
- 10 cloves garlic
- Fresh ground pepper
- 2 tbsp. dry mustard
- 1/4th tsp. hot pepper flakes

- ½ tsp cinnamon
- ½ cup red wine vinegar

Directions:

4. Rub down the ribs with the cloves pepper and cinnamon on both sides. Place the ribs on the smoking rack
5. Smoke ribs in the smoker for 6 hours with apple wood chips until tender or internal temp of 170 degrees °F.
6. Mix in all the barbeque sauce ingredients and simmer on low heat, covered for 1 hour. Stir occasionally while adding vinegar to taste. Allow to simmer for 15 additional minutes. Place in the refrigerator until cool.

Simple Smoked Chicken

(ready in about 6 hours | Serving 8)

Ingredients:

- Chicken 3 to 3.5 lb.
- 1 gallon water
- Oak wood chips
- 1 cup sugar
- 1 cup salt
- Any other spices or liquid sauces you may want to add.

Directions:

7. Place the salt, sugar and any other spices you may want in the gallon of water. Place the chicken in the water and let sit for 4 hours. Remove the chicken and rinse the brine off.
8. You can now season your chicken any way you want and place in a smoker breast side down, holding a temperature of 225 °F with oak chips as a wood base.
9. Place hickory in on the oak to give it more flavor. Cook the chicken for 1 ½ hours. Remove the chicken when internal temperature reaches 140 °F.

Deep Smoked Meatloaf

(ready in about 4 hours | Serving 8)

Ingredients:

- 2 lbs. ground beef
- ½ green pepper, finely chopped
- 1 onion, chopped finely
- 1 cup bread crumbs
- 2 cloves garlic, minced
- 3/4th cup ketchup
- 2 eggs lightly beaten
- 1/4th cup milk

Directions:

1. Blend all ingredients into a bowl until well mixed. Place the mixture on a cookie sheet and mold into a form.

2. Place in the smoker with any flavored wood chips you want at 250 °F for 3 to 4 hours. Add ketchup or barbeque sauce the last 30 minutes before finishing. Make sure the internal temperature registers at 150 °F.

Grand Texas Smoked Brisket

(ready in about 1 ½ day | Serving 8 to 10)

Ingredients:

- Wood chips of your flavor
- 1/4th cup sugar
- 1/4th cup paprika
- 1/4th cup cayenne pepper
- 1/4th cup ground cumin
- 1/4th cup chili powder
- 1/4th cup brown sugar
- 1/4th cup onion powder
- 1/4th cup garlic powder
- 1/4th cup fresh cracked black pepper
- 1/4th cup salt
- 10 lbs. of beef brisket

Directions:

8. Place wood chips in a bowl with water to soak for 8 hours.
9. In a bowl mix sugar, paprika, cayenne pepper, cumin, chili powder, brown sugar, onion powder, garlic powder, black pepper and salt together.
10. Preheat your smoker at 220 F°. Drain the water from your wood chips and place them in your smoker.
11. Place the brisket in the smoker and let smoke for 12 ½ hours or until the temperature inside reaches 165 °F. Remove and wrap tightly in heavy-duty aluminum foil. Return the brisket to the smoker.
12. Cook for an additional 1 hour or until internal temperature reaches 185 °F

Prime Maple-Smoked Rib

(ready in about 1 hour 30 minutes | Serving 5 to 6)

Ingredients:

- 1 (6 lb.) rib roast, 3 rib standing, bones separated and tied back in place.
- 3 cups maple wood chips
- Sea salt to taste
- Coarse ground black pepper to taste

Directions:

1. Place wood chips in a bowl of water for 1 hour until moistened completely.
2. Preheat your smoker to be 225 °F and hang the drip pan on the rack beneath the area where the meat will be.
3. Coat the roast with salt and pepper working it in with your hands.

4. Place the roast fat side up into the preheated smoker.
5. Place 2/3 cup of the wood chips into the smoker
6. Smoke the roast for 30 minutes and add half of the wood chips that are remaining. Smoke for 30 more minutes and add the last half of the wood chips. Smoke for about 2 more hours or until the internal temperature reaches 125 °F.
7. Remove the roast and let it rest for 30 minutes before carving ½ to 1 inch thick slices.

Smoked Pork Spare Ribs
(ready in about 12 hours | Serving 6)

Ingredients:

- 2 Tbsps. Chili powder
- ½ cup packed brown sugar
- 1 tbsp. black pepper
- 1 tbsp. paprika
- 2 tsp. onion powder
- 2 tbsps. Garlic powder
- 2 tsps. Ground cumin
- 2 tsps. Salt
- 1 tsp. jalapeno seasoning salt
- 1 tsp. ground cinnamon
- 1 tsp. cayenne pepper
- ¾ cup apple cider vinegar
- 1 cup apple cider
- 1 tbsp. garlic powder
- 1 tbsp. onion powder

- 1 jalapeno pepper, finely chopped
- 2 tbsps. Lemon juice
- Kosher salt and ground black pepper to taste
- 3 tbsps. Hot pepper sauce
- 2 cups wood chips, soaked
- 6 lbs. pork spareribs

Directions:

5. Mix the first 11 ingredients in a bowl together and rub the mixture on the spare ribs. Make sure to coat them completely, cover and refrigerate for 4 hours.
6. Preheat your charcoal grill for 250 °F.
7. In a medium bowl mix the remaining ingredients not including the ribs.
8. Place 2 handfuls of wood chips on the now grayed charcoal. Lay the ribs out on the grill bone down. Close the grill and cook for 3 ½ to 4 hours. Add additional coals as you need them. Baste the ribs with the sauce and add a handful of woodchips every hour. Try to keep the temperature of the grill above 225 °F. The ribs will be done when the seasoning has become crispy and blackened. Also the meat will have pulled away from the bone

Carolina-Style Pulled Pork

(ready in about 15 hours | Serving 10)

Ingredients:

- 2 tsps. Light brown sugar
- 1 tbsp. mild paprika
- ½ tsp. celery salt
- 1 ½ tsps. hot paprika
- ½ tsp. dry mustard
- ½ tsp. garlic salt
- ½ tsp. onion powder
- ½ tsp. ground black pepper
- ¼ tsp. salt
- 1 1/3rd cups water
- 2 cups cider vinegar
- ¼ cup firmly packed brown sugar
- 5/8th cup ketchup
- 4 tsps. Crushed red pepper flakes

- 5 tsps. Salt
- 1 tsp. ground white pepper
- 1 tsp. ground black pepper.
- 2 lbs. hickory wood chips, soaked
- 8 lbs. pork butt roast

Directions:

10. Mix the first 9 ingredients into a small bowl and rub all over the roast. Wrap the roast in plastic wrap and refrigerate for 8 hours.
11. Preheat the grill at 225 °F and wait until coals become grayed over. When the coals gray over place a handful of wood chips on them. Place the pork butt roast on the grill over the drip pan. Close the grill and cook for 12 hours adding a handful of wood chips every hour. Also add coal as needed.
12. While the pork butt is smoking mix the last 8 ingredients not including the pork butt and wood chips into a medium bowl. Whisk the ingredients until they turn brown.
13. Remove the pork butt roast and start shredding. When the pork is shredded mix it in with the sauce you created

Smokehouse Beef Jerky

(ready in about 14 hours | Serving 1 lb.)

Ingredients:

- 1 cup Worcestershire sauce
- 2 cups soy sauce
- 1 cup teriyaki sauce
- 1 cup cranberry-grape juice
- 2 tbsp. steak sauce
- 1 tbsp. hot pepper sauce
- ½ tsp. ground black pepper, to taste
- 1 cup light brown sugar
- 4 cups wood chips, or as needed
- 2 lbs. flank steak, sliced into ¼ inch slices against the grain

Directions:

7. Whisk the first 8 ingredients together and pour into a reseal able plastic bag. Place the sliced meat in the bag and press out the air before sealing it. Place the bag in the refrigerator and let it marinade for 8 to 10 hours.

8. With the smoker at 170 °F, remove the slices of steak and place on the rack of the smoker and add the wood chips. Smoke for about 6 to 8 hours adding a handful of wood chips every hour.

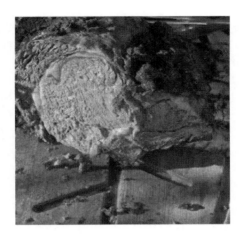

Smoked Standing Rib Roast

(ready in about 10hours | Serving 6)

Ingredients:

- 15 pounds charcoal briquettes
- 2 pounds hickory wood chips
- 1 cup bourbon whiskey
- 1 (4 pound) rib roast, bone intact
- ½ cup steak seasoning

Directions:

1. Start 10 pounds of charcoal, torpedo style smoker. Start a hot fire, fill secondary pan with cold water and allow coals to turn white. Soak hickory chips in bourbon. Rub roast with the steak seasoning, ensuring that all surfaces are coated.
2. Once the coals are ready, place the roast on the top grate. Throw numerous handfuls of soaked hickorychips into the fire, close the lid. Check fire regularly every 45 minutes, add more charcoal to keep flame alive. Cook for 8-10 hours, meat should be 145 degrees F in the center once finished.

Smoked Steelhead Trout Salmon

(ready in about 13 hours | Servings 6)

Ingredients:

- 2 pounds steelhead trout fillets
- 2 tbsp. olive oil
- 4 chopped garlic cloves
- 1 ½ tbsp. dried rosemary, crushed
- 1 cup sugar-based curing mixture
- 1 quarter of water
- Ground black pepper
- 1 pound alder wood chips, soaked in wine or water

Directions:
1. Rinse fish fillets and place in shallow (preferably glass) baking dish. Drizzle oil over the fish and season with

rosemary and garlic. Rub seasonings well into the fish. Cover and chill overnight

2. Dissolve curing salt in water and pour into shallow dish, fish intact. Allow to marinate for 15 minutes.

3. Prepare the smoker to operate for 4 hours on slow burn, use charcoal. Temperature should be at 150 degrees F prior to cooking.

4. Transfer fish from brine and cover each piece with aluminum foil, season with pepper for tasting. Place each piece onto rack and sprinkle soaked wood chips over the coal. Cover and smoke for 2 hours, replenish if required.

5. Increase temperature to 200 degrees F and continue to smoke until internal temperature of fish reaches 165 degrees F. Remove from smoker, rest for 20 minutes and serve.

Smoked Pork Butt

(ready in about 1 day 12 hours 20 mins | Servings 16)

Ingredients:

- 7 pounds of fresh pork butt roast
- 2 tbsp. ground New Mexico chile powder
- 4 tbsp. brown sugar, packed

Directions:

1. Soak pork butt in brine solution for 4 hours (or overnight), covered in the refrigerator
2. Preheat outdoor smoker to 200-225 degrees F
3. Use a small bowl to combine brown sugar, chili powder and additional seasoning, if desired. Apply to the meat and season well, rubbing in with your fingers. Allocate roasting rack above a drip pan and transfer meat to the rack

4. Smoke at 200-225 degrees F for 6-18 hours, depending on preference. Internal heat of pork should reach 145 degrees F prior to completion

Honey Smoked Turkey

(ready in about 3 hours 45 minutes | Servings 1 (12pound) turkey)

Ingredients:

- 1 whole turkey
- 2 tbsp. fresh sage, chopped
- 2tbsp. ground black pepper
- 2 tbsp. celery salt
- 2 tbsp. fresh basil, chopped
- 2 tbsp. vegetable oil
- 1 (12 ounce) jar of honey
- ½ pound of mesquite wood chips

Directions:

1. Preheat grill to high heat. If using charcoal grill, use twice the regular amount. Soak wood chips in water and place next to grill

2. Remove giblets and neck from turkey. Rinse well and pat dry. Transfer to a large roasting pan.
3. Mix together black pepper, sage, basil, celery salt and vegetable oil in a medium bowl. Pour mixture over turkey evenly. Place the turkey breast side down into the pan, tent and cover with aluminum foil.
4. Move roasting pan into the preheated grill. Throw handfuls of wood chips into the coals. Cover and cook for 1 hour.
5. Throw 2 more handfuls of wood chips into the fire. Drizzle honey over the turkey and replace the foil. Cover grill and cook for further 1 ½-2 hours. Internal temperature should reach 180 degrees F.
6. Remove foil from turkey and turn breast side up in roasting pan. Baste with any leftover honey and allow to cook, uncovered, for 15 minutes. Serve once honey is very dark.

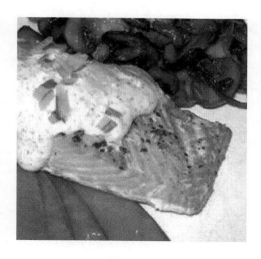

Alder Pan Smoked Salmon
(ready in about 10 hours | Serving 10)

Ingredients:

- 1 (3 pound) salmon fillet
- Fresh ground black pepper
- 1/8 cup brown sugar, packed
- ½ tsp. salt
- 1 tbsp. water

Directions:
1. Soak salmon fillet in premade brine solution for 4 hours, or overnight. Submerge alder wood plank in water.
2. Preheat outdoor smoker to 160-180 degrees F.
3. Transfer salmon from brine to cold running water, rinse well. Pat dry and remove wood plank from water, lay fish onto the plank. Season with black pepper.

4. Smoke salmon for 2 hours, check at 1 ½ hours just in case. Fish should be able to flake into pieces. Adjust cooking time based on the amount of reduction of salt content during cooking, as salt content diminishes over time.
5. 30 minutes before fish is done, mix brown sugar and water to form paste. Brush over the salmon and serve.

Mouth Watering Beef Jerky
(ready in about 18 hours | Serving 12)

Ingredients:

- 5 pounds boneless beef sirloin
- 2 cups soy sauce
- 1 cup water
- 3 dashes Worcestershire sauce
- 3 tbsp. white sugar (optional)
- 3 tbsp. salt
- ½ tsp. onion powder
- ¼ tsp. garlic powder
- 2 tsp. liquid smoke flavoring
- Mesquite or hickory wood chips

Directions:
1. Cut beef into ¼ inch thick slices. In a small bowl combine water, soy sauce, Worcestershire sauce, salt, sugar, garlic

powder, onion powder and liquid smoke. Pour mixture into heavy duty re-sealable bag. Add beef and combine well; seal and chill for 12 hours

2. Remove beef from bag and pat dry, allow to sit for 30 minutes. Discard marinade and soak wood chips in preparation for cooking
3. Preheat smoker prior to cooking
4. Arrange beef into drying racks. Smoke for 5-7 hours, replenish wood chips when required.

Crispy Grilled Pizza Margherita
(ready in about 1 hour 35 minutes | Serving 6)

Ingredients:

- 1 (16 ounce) pizza dough package, room temperature
- ¼ cup olive oil
- 4ounces shredded Asiago cheese
- 3 thinly sliced large tomatoes
- 1 cup whole basil leaves, packed
- 8 ounces fresh mozzarella cheese, shredded
- Salt and black pepper, for tasting

Directions:

14. Preheat outdoor grill to high heat, oil the grate lightly
15. Place pizza dough into a bowl and allow to rise 2-3 times its original size, approx. 1 hour. Flour flat surface area

and divide dough in half; roll each section to 10-12 inch diameter circle

16. Place pizza rounds onto a preheated grill, use a wooden paddle and cover; cook until grill marks start to appear at the bottom, approx. 3-5 minutes. Transfer from grill and flip over onto work surface. Low grill temperature to medium.

17. Brush each round with oil. Place half of Asiago cheese onto each crust; add basil, tomatoes and mozzarella cheese. Season with salt and pepper.

18. Transfer pizzas to grill and close the lid. Cook until cheese is melted and bottom rounds produce grill marks, approx. 7-10 minutes. Remove from heat and allow to sit for 5 minutes prior to serving.

Grilled Zucchini

(ready in about 30minutes | Serving 2)

Ingredients:

- 1 large zucchini
- 4 tbsp. butter
- Salt and pepper

Directions:

9. Preheat grill to medium temperature
10. Clean exterior of the zucchini, slice into lengthwise quarters. Place pieces of butter onto each zucchini quarter, season with salt and pepper for flavor. Wrap each quarter in aluminum foil.
11. Place foil wraps onto heated grill and cook for 10-15 minutes on each side.

Smoked Asparagus

(ready in about 1 hour 30 minutes | Serving 1 ½ pounds asparagus)

Ingredients:

- 2 tbsp. of butter
- 4 thinly sliced garlic cloves
- 2 tbsp. lemon juice
- Salt
- ¼ tsp. ground black pepper
- 1 thinly sliced onion
- 1 ½ pounds of trimmed asparagus

Directions:

1. Place charcoal on bottom pan of the smoker. Light coals and allow temperature to rise to 240 degrees F.

2. Melt butter into a small saucepan, stir in garlic and cook over low heat. Remove from heat and combine lemon juice, salt and pepper
3. Place onions into bottom of large cast iron skillet. Spread asparagus over onions. Drizzle garlic mixture and butter over asparagus. Place uncovered skillet (or preferred baking dish) onto the top grate of preheated smoker.
4. Close smoker and cook for 1 hour.

Smoked Herb Chicken

(ready in about 4 hours | Serving 1 chicken)

Ingredients:

- 1 (4 pound) whole chicken
- 3 tbsp. butter
- 1 tbsp. fresh parsley, chopped
- 1 tbsp. fresh oregano, chopped
- 1 tbsp. fresh basil, chopped
- 1 tbsp. fresh chives, finely chopped

Directions:

1. Preheat outdoor grill on low temperature.
2. Rinse chicken inside and out. Pat dry and loosen skin around breast region.

3. Place 3 tbsp. of butter in various regions under the skin. Combine herbs and place half under skin, other half directly inside the chicken.
4. Cook chicken and smoke for 3 hours, juices should run clear once poked with a fork.

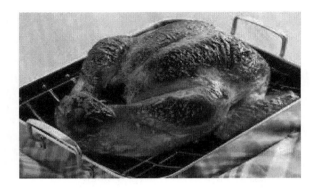

Comely Honey Turkey
(ready in about 12 hours 30 minutes | Serving 1 whole turkey)

Ingredients:

- 1 lb. salt
- 1 gallon hot water
- 2 (8 oz.) jars honey
- 2 qt. vegetable broth
- 1 (7 lb.) bag of ice
- 1 cup orange juice
- 1/4th cup vegetable oil
- 1 (15 lb.) Whole turkey, giblets and neck removed
- 1 granny smith apple, cored and cut
- 1 tsp. poultry seasoning
- 1 small onion, cut into chunks
- 1 stalk celery, cut into chunks
- 1 orange, quartered

Directions:

1. Using a large container mix salt in with water and stir until dissolved. Mix honey, vegetable broth, and orange juice. Pour the ice cubes into the brine and add the turkey afterwards so that it is breast up. Close the lid and let sit in a cold (under 40 °F) place for 12 hours.
2. Remove the turkey and dry thoroughly using a paper towel. Use a bowl to mix poultry seasoning and vegetable oil. Rub the mixture all over the turkey and place celery, apple, orange, and onion into the turkey's cavity.
3. Preheat the grill to 400 °F and place the turkey on a lightly oiled grate. Place 1 cup of the hickory wood chips to begin smoking process.
4. Grill the turkey for 1 hour on indirect heat. Check the center to see if it reaches 160 °F. Apply foil over the turkey and add more wood chips every hour cooking for an additional 2 to 3 hours. Check again for the internal temperature of 160 °F. If internal temperature has been reached, remove from the grill and let rest for 1 hour.

Your Free Gift

I wanted to show my appreciation that you support my work so I've put together a free gift for you.

Slowcooker Essentials Cookbook

http://thezenfactory.com/51_recipes_free_book
/

Just visit the link above to download it now.

I know you will love this gift.

Thanks!

Conclusion

The amazing taste of smoked meat, no matter what type, gives everyone a homey feeling that can bring back amazing memories of their childhood and create new memories with friends, family and associates.

The power of smoked meat has the ability take you back to a place where you are happy, free, and comfortable. This is why you can never underestimate the power of food and the way it is cooked.

It has been proven that people are happier and more active in the summer months. Ironically, this is also when people seem to spend more time out in the sun and socializing with the people they love. It is also the time where most people break out the smokers and begin smoking meat and having barbecues.

We hope you have enjoyed the simple, yet delicious recipes that are contained in this book. The amazing flavor of each of these recipes will have you enjoying the summer, or even the winter months.

Made in the USA
Middletown, DE
12 December 2016